Canny Granny
How to Be the Favorite Grandparent

Elizabeth Gardner

Copyright © 2007 and © 2021 Elizabeth Gardner
SECOND EDITION All rights reserved.
ISBN-13: 9798726668338
No portion of this book may be reproduced in any form without permission from the author, except as permitted by U.S. copyright law. Every effort has been made by the author and publishing house to ensure that the information contained in this book was correct as of press time. The author and publisher hereby disclaim and do not assume liability for any injury, loss, damage, or disruption caused by errors or omissions, regardless of whether errors or omissions result from negligence, accident, or any other cause. Readers are encouraged to verify any information contained in this book prior to taking any action on the information. For rights and permissions, please contact:
Elizabeth Gardner neonpinklime@gmail.com

Contents

Chapter One Get Ready for Grandbaby 1

Chapter Two Help at Birth and with the Newborn 8

Chapter Three Maintain a Good Relationship with Mom & Dad . 12

Chapter Four Get More Visits 16

Chapter Five Increase Birthday, Holiday, and
Special Occasion Visits 21

Chapter Six When Things are too Good at Grandma's
How to Get Less Visits 26

Chapter Seven Long-Distance Grandparenting 29

Chapter Eight Create Meaningful Shared Experiences 35

Chapter Nine Thoughtful Gifts that Resonate 41

Chapter Ten Stay the Favorite 46

About the Author 48

Chapter One

Get Ready for Grandbaby

1. Use specific suggestions when offering help. (See 3-10 below)

2. Remind mom and dad that they can ask your advice.

3. Offer to babysit.

4. Offer to pick kids up from school and/or take them to afterschool activities.

5. Offer to do some housecleaning or run errands.

6. Invite the family to your home for lunch or dinner.

7. Make meals to give to the family.

8. Offer to help with a baby shower.

9. Offer to help address/mail birth announcements.

10. Pitch in for baby items.

Every grandparent wants to be the favorite. Favorites learn good and bad news first, enjoy grandkid texts and calls, help at school and afterschool activities, share more holiday time, plan birthday celebrations, linger with mom and dad over coffee and dessert, enjoy grandkid outings, and host sleepovers. How do you become the favorite? What's the secret?

1. Use specific suggestions when offering help.

A new grandchild! When is the baby due? Will it be a boy or a girl? What will the name be? How can I help?

Grandparents want to help anyway they can and often feel frustrated when they can't do more. "I want to help, but when I ask what they need, they politely refuse" or "I've tried to help, but they're so busy it's hard to pin them down" or "I'd like to be more involved in baby preparations, but I don't know what more I can do," and then there's the all too common, "Call me if you need anything"—and they never do.

Remember what it was like when you were expecting a baby? From an emotional and physical standpoint, not much has changed. Sure, now there's a ton of high-tech baby gear like SUV strollers, disposable diaper units, video monitors, etc., but the emotional and physical turmoil families experience remain the same. Remember the swirl of excitement, morning sickness, bills, sleepless nights, preparing the siblings, and doctor visits? It's a nine-month period of adjustment continuing after baby arrives—don't be put off by what they say and do. Mom and dad need you and your experience now more than ever.

While you're afraid of butting in, mom and dad are afraid of imposing on you.

Most moms and dads refuse help because of politeness and pride. They don't want to burden others with their problems, so they refuse offers of help with a polite, knee-jerk response like "we're fine" or "we don't need anything." In our society, these polite refusals are so customary that they're automatically uttered without any real thought, and moms and dads worry that if they ask for or accept offers of help, others will think they can't handle being parents. So, while you're worried about being "too pushy" or "butting in" with offers of help, they're worried about imposing on you and what you'll think of them as parents, and, making matters worse, some parents view offers to help as an effort to be polite without any real intention to help. What can grandparents do?

Offer specific help. Vague or broad offers are politely and easily refused with little consideration. On the other hand, specific suggestions (1) stop, in a nonconfrontational way, that annoying knee-jerk response of polite refusal by making expectant or new parents consider specific possibilities; (2) help expectant or new parents cut through their tired and busy minds by providing a road map of help which makes them consider options they hadn't before; and (3) are more likely to be accepted because they took time and thought to formulate—conveying that it's a sincere offer of help.

How best to offer help? Begin your conversation with an open-ended offer like "How can I help?" but don't stop there. You'll probably receive the polite "Oh no that's okay, we're fine" response. Answer their polite refusal with a specific suggestion like, "How about I pick up the older kids from school twice a week?" or "Maybe I could help with the baby shower, can I have the phone number of the person who's throwing it?" or "Maybe after baby is born, I could come over in the afternoons for a week and babysit, so you can get some rest or run errands?" There are lots of possibilities. Use the list at the beginning of this chapter for ideas. Refer to it when you call mom and dad or use it to jot down your own specific suggestions. If they refuse your more specific offers of help, then don't push. Accept their "no" and try again another time.

> *Specific offers of help make mom and dad consider new possibilities, provide a road map of help and convey sincerity.*

Above all, don't be offended or upset. Parents are busy and distracted and most times that's all it is. If you get upset, you'll be less likely to try again or end up getting into an argument with mom or dad. A little pressure offering specific suggestions of help now and again is reasonable but getting angry and upset will make mom and dad recoil from you.

2. Remind mom and dad that they can ask your advice.

Understandably, parents are overwhelmed. They may not yet realize what they need or how you can help. In the exhausting swirl of excitement before and after baby's birth, it's easy for mom and dad to forget that their own parents went through this and can be a wonderful source of comfort and help. Combine that with the belief that they should do as much as they can by themselves without burdening others, and it's not surprising that parents forget that their own parents are a wonderful source of advice and inspiration. Give them a gentle reminder every now and then that you've been through this and your experienced guidance is at the ready.

> *Picking up grandkids from school is a big help to mom and dad.*

3. Offer to babysit.

Babysitting baby and/or older brothers and sisters is a big help. Babysit them at their home or take them to the park, mall, out to lunch, or to your home. Even a short break can go a long way to rejuvenating mom or dad, and, of course, seeing your grandkids more often is a big plus for you. If your schedule allows, you may want to offer a weekly babysit day. Make sure mom and dad leave a phone number where they can be reached as well as a list of emergency numbers to call if there's a problem.

> *If your schedule allows, you may want to offer a weekly babysit day.*

4. Offer to pick kids up from school and/or take them to afterschool activities.

If you're able, offer to pick kids up from school. Even once or twice a week is a big help. While out running errands, mom and dad must be ever mindful to return to school for pick up. That means dashing from one appointment to the next hoping there's enough time. Then there's the mad dash to the school itself. If there isn't enough parking, being late can mean a long walk for a pregnant mom.

Once when I was dropping my two older boys off at school, I was late and in a rush. While holding their hands crossing a street, I fell, and they went down with me. Luckily, they were unharmed, but I suffered ripped pants, a skinned knee, and the embarrassment of being a large pregnant woman sprawled out in front of morning commuters. It was a sign that I needed to slow down.

To help, my mother-in-law and husband agreed that he'd drop the kids off in the morning on his way to work, and she'd pick them up in the afternoon. At first, I refused saying it wasn't necessary because I didn't want to burden grandma, but they insisted. After a few days, I realized how calm and rested I felt. It turned out to be a great idea.

Consider also that if your grandkids are like most kids, then they have lots of afterschool activities. The days you remember when parents could safely let kids bike and play unsupervised in the neighborhood are gone and replaced with supervised activities. Ask mom and dad if you can take grandkids to soccer or baseball practice? Maybe a lift to ballet or gymnastics would help? Mom and dad would undoubtedly welcome your help transporting grandchildren to whatever activity you choose. Watching the activity while waiting to take them home is great fun and will provide lots of opportunity for quality discussion. Besides, grandkids love to show off and make grandma and grandpa proud.

5. Offer to do some housecleaning or run errands.

This is particularly helpful when both parents work and/or mom is tired or sick from pregnancy. When you go to the grocery store, ask mom and dad what they need, or suggest running a vacuum around their home once a week or doing a couple of loads of laundry? Perhaps you could take older kids to little league, soccer practice, ballet, or a music lesson? There are lots of ways to help mom and dad while also increasing your involvement in your grandchildren's lives.

6. Invite the family to your home for lunch or dinner.

When both parents work and/or one is tired or sick from pregnancy, preparing three healthy meals a day for the family can seem like an insurmountable task. Give mom and dad a break by inviting them over to your place for lunch or dinner. Remember though that with young children it can be difficult to go out due to nap schedules, diapers, special food requirements like formula or toddler finger foods, highchair, etc., so you may find parents reluctant to accept your offer. Having those items on hand will make it easier for them to come over. See chapter four "Getting More Visits" for ways to make your home more comfortable for a young family.

> *Making meals and delivering them to the new family no strings attached is greatly appreciated. Drop one off every so often.*

7. Make meals to give to the family.

Grandparents and great grandparents have done this for me, and it's a life saver! What makes this so great is that you don't need to ask permission. Just make the meal and drop it off. The new family can eat it that night or freeze to use another day. When you're tired or sick from pregnancy, not having to cook for the family is much appreciated.

8. Offer to help with a baby shower.

If the expectant parents don't have anyone throwing them a shower, you may want to volunteer. If they do, ask for the person's name and phone number so you can call and offer help. Some couples throw their own shower. If so, offer to bring food or drink, set up, clean up, or address invitations.

9. Offer to help address/mail birth announcements.

This is one task for which grandparents are especially helpful because they've got addresses for extended family members and friends that expectant parents don't. When I was expecting my first child, I called my mother and mother-in-law and asked them each to create a list with addresses of relatives and friends that they thought should receive a birth announcement. That helped me identify persons I might have missed, and I didn't have to call around to hunt down addresses. Don't forget to offer help addressing and stuffing envelopes. With a new baby at home, it can be hard to get those announcements out the door.

10. Pitch in for baby items.

Ask mom and dad if there's anything they'd like for baby that you could help with, for example, crib, stroller, car seat, breast pump, changing table, highchair, baby front/backpack. These necessities can run upwards of $100 dollars each, and mom and dad might be reluctant to ask for help. Also, canny grannies know that an offer to purchase baby items will almost certainly lead to a shopping trip with mom and dad. Offer to help and shop. Share in the fun!

Chapter Two

Help at Birth and with the Newborn

1. Offer to babysit grandkids on the day of birth.

2. Offer live-in help.

3. Offer to babysit after baby is born.

4. Bring food, coffee, meals.

5. Offer to do housework.

6. Offer to run errands.

Birth is an exciting time, and of course you want to help however you can. You'll most likely want to be at the hospital or homebirth to share in the joy of welcoming the newest family member. Will you be babysitting an expectant big brother or sister at home or in the hospital waiting room? Can you get yourself to the hospital? Will you be making meals or taking

> *Baby could come early. Months before the due date, make sure everyone understands what to do the day baby is born.*

siblings to/from school on the day of the birth? Are you going to live-in and help care for baby for a few weeks? Numbers 2-7 at the beginning of this chapter suggest specific ways to help mom and dad.

1. Offer to babysit grandkids on the day of birth.

Mom and dad will most likely need a babysitter for big brother or sister during delivery. If you agree to babysit, it may mean that you won't be present at the birth but arrive sometime later with big brother or sister to see the new baby. Discuss the possibilities with mom and dad. Make sure you're all happy and secure with the plan. If you need to make meals, pickup/drop-off at school, tuck grandkids into bed, etc., discuss with mom and dad what you'll need in order to do that.

> *Driving yourself or riding with a relative to the hospital decreases stress on mom and dad allowing them to focus on the birth.*

2. Offer live-in help.

If you're able to take a week or two off to live-in and help the new family, then offer. While researching *Crib Sheets New Parent Sleep Solutions,* new moms repeatedly told me that having grandma or another relative live-in to help was a real lifesaver. Newborns feed every two hours which means at least one parent will be up through the night. It's exhausting.

I didn't have live-in help with my first baby, and I was exhausted. The second time around, I had a toddler to look after and couldn't sleep when baby sleeps, so great grandma moved in for three weeks to help. What a difference she made. I'd be up with baby every two hours through the night. At 8 a.m., great grandma would wake and take baby for four hours, so I could get some sleep. If I hadn't pumped, then I wouldn't get the full four hours, but grandma did her best to placate baby as long as possible. She also fixed breakfast for my toddler and kept him entertained.

> *If another relative is living in, suggest a schedule of day visits after they leave.*

The schedule we came up with made such a difference for me physically and mentally. Physically, I was able to get more sleep which helped mentally because I was happier and more patient. But the best psychological boost came when managing a crying baby at two or three in the morning; it was much easier to get through the frustration knowing that at 8 a.m. I'd get a break.

Discuss the possibility of living-in with mom and dad before baby arrives. Some couples arrange to have relatives live with them different weeks after birth—a schedule of live-in help.

3. Offer to babysit after baby is born.

If living with the family for a week or two isn't possible, then consider a week or two of day visits. One grandma told me that since mom and dad already had live-in help, she offered day visits after their live-in help left. She babysat her six-week-old grandson for four hours during the afternoons for a week. This allowed mom to run errands, catch up on sleep, and get ready to go back to her full-time job. It also allowed grandma to bond with her new grandson without turning her life upside down or interrupt her work schedule, as living-in would.

4. Bring food, coffee, meals.

As discussed in chapter one, this is always appreciated. Proper nutrition is especially important if mom is breastfeeding. Unfortunately, the demands of a newborn make it difficult for parents to eat well-balanced meals. Stop over with a meal, fruit, or coffee. Do it no strings attached—hand over the food and leave. Explain that you'll call them for a visit when things calm down.

I remember when friends of ours had their first baby. I made spaghetti and brought it to their apartment. When the exhausted dad came to the door, I handed him the spaghetti and left. Weeks later, he called to say that they ate the spaghetti in their pajamas. They were grateful that I simply handed them the meal and left.

5. Offer to do housework.

When there's a newborn at home, parents have little energy to do anything but sleep and eat. Explain that you realize how busy they are and offer to do light housework like vacuuming or laundry.

6. Offer to run errands.

Offer to get groceries or bring older children to/from school. Maybe you could walk the dog or pick up a package from the post office? How about picking up a prescription or fast food for dinner? When you ask if there's anything they need, cut through their foggy, sleep deprived minds with specific suggestions.

Chapter Three

Maintain a Good Relationship with Mom and Dad

1. Give your opinion but respect mom and dad's decisions.

2. Deal with your own relatives.

3. Offer specific suggestions to change what you don't like.

When it comes to rearing children, the tension that exists between parents and grandparents is present in each generation. Maybe you think your grandkids are drinking too much soda and not enough milk, or you don't believe they have a reasonable bed time? Perhaps you don't agree with the religious faith with which they'll be raised, or maybe you think your pregnant daughter-in-law shouldn't go back to work after the baby is born? Alternatively, maybe mom and dad think you spoil their kids too much, or perhaps they think you interfere with your opinions? It's a push and pull as parents and grandparents define their roles. Once a new baby arrives, however, sleep deprived parents can easily lose patience and tact. Emotions are in flux and tempers short as everyone adjusts to the new edition.

> *When it comes to maintaining good relations with mom and dad, remember: Give your opinion but always respect their decisions.*

1. **Give your opinion but respect mom and dad's decisions.**

Grandparents are thrilled to be grandparents but also relieved not to be parents. "Been there, done that," one proud grandpa told me, "Now it's their turn." One of the biggest joys of grandparenting is having fun with your grandkids and then going home. You're not responsible for raising them, but that also means you don't decide how they are raised. Because you care deeply about your kids and their children, you'll have opinions about your grandkids' upbringing. You've got a lot of experience and wisdom to offer, but prepare yourself for the fact that mom and dad will not always follow your advice.

When it comes to maintaining good relations with mom and dad, there's one simple rule to remember: give your opinion but respect their decisions. If you don't respect their decisions, it will lead to distrust and arguments resulting in less time with your grandkids. Remember how your own parents behaved when you set rules for your kids? Were you upset when grandma or grandpa gave them a toy after you said no, or fed them goodies before dinner? How did you feel when grandma or grandpa spanked even though you told them you'd handle discipline? I'm sure you can think of instances in your own parenting past where your wishes were ignored by grandma or grandpa.

2. **Deal with your own relatives.**

This is the best way to prevent arguments. I'm talking about avoiding family feuds. In my book *Crib Sheets New Parent Sleep Solutions,* I discuss the same rule from the parents' perspective. I explain that it's best to discuss extended family, birth arrangements, holiday plans, religion, and other difficult issues with your blood relatives

> *To prevent argument, discuss difficult matters with your blood relative, i.e., your son or daughter, not your son-in-law or daughter-in-law.*

because, for example, no matter what you say to your parents, they'll still love you. Therefore, when unpleasant or uncomfortable matters must be discussed with extended family, deal with your own parents or relatives and let your spouse deal with theirs.

Ditto from the grandparents' perspective. If you have a difficult issue to discuss, then discuss it with your son or daughter, not an in-law. Let your son or daughter discuss it with their spouse. Limit discussions with your daughter-in-law or son-in-law to pleasant conversations and babysitting arrangements.

3. **Offer specific suggestions to change what you don't like.**

Okay, you have to be careful here. You've identified something you don't like regarding the raising of your grandkids. You've talked to your blood relative son or daughter, and they've decided that they're going to continue doing whatever it is you don't like. One last thing you could try is to raise the issue again with your son or daughter by offering specific suggestions of what they could do instead. This may cause them to consider possibilities they hadn't before, but be prepared for the probability that they may still disagree and continue doing whatever it is you don't like. At that point, you should respect their decision as parents.

Here's an example of how this can work. When I was weaning my third child off formula, she drank watered down juice from a sippy cup at meals. My mother-in-law, her grandma, didn't like that. Now, rather than telling her son (telling a blood relative helps to decrease argument) she told me, her daughter-in-law, that she didn't agree. She thought I should feed milk with meals. I repeatedly explained that I'd tried to do that, but the baby didn't like the taste (baby formula tastes different from cow's milk). Grandma was disappointed in me. I was unhappy because I felt like she was thinking I wasn't a good mom.

One day while she watched the baby, she gave her milk with her meal. This annoyed me because she deliberately went against my wishes, but she discovered that the baby did indeed refuse cow's milk. She dropped the subject for a week. Then, she reapproached me with a specific suggestion. She suggested that I heat the milk to warm it up for baby. I did, and baby drank it. I hadn't thought to heat it up. Now I give my baby either milk or juice with meals.

As I discussed in chapter one of this book, there are some distinct advantages to offering specific suggestions that make them more likely to be accepted. Specific suggestions (1) stop that annoying knee-jerk, polite-refusal reaction in a nonconfrontational way by causing parents to consider specific possibilities they hadn't before; (2) help parents cut through their tired, and busy minds by providing a road map of help; and (3) are more likely to be accepted because they convey sincerity.

Chapter Four

Get More Visits

1. Keep a kid friendly home.
2. Provide changing area with diapers and wipes.
3. Provide baby formula and bottle.
4. Provide a safe sleeping area for baby, e.g., Moses' basket, bassinet, or playpen, with baby monitor.
5. Provide toys for baby and older siblings.
6. Be ready to pick up and drop off grandkids.
7. Offer a meal.

Parents are busy juggling work, school, housework, afterschool activities, and homework schedules. Throw in scheduled and unscheduled nap times for baby and bottle or breastfeeding and you've got a hectic schedule that's neither predictable nor flexible. That's why the easier it is for mom and dad to bring their kids over to grandma's for a visit, the more they will. This chapter will help you make your home more kid friendly, so you get more visits.

1. Keep a kid friendly home.

My family is fortunate to have grandparents and great grandparents living nearby. My kids visit their grandparents more often because their house is kid friendly. It's just easier at grandma's than it is at great grandma's.

At great grandma's house, fragile items are within reach on coffee and side tables. The carpet isn't well vacuumed and baby has put bits in her mouth and found loose sewing needles. Electrical outlets don't have covers, and there aren't kid snacks which means I must bring them or feed the kids before visiting, and, there's no highchair, so I carefully time the visit so baby is full when we arrive. There's no safe place for baby to sleep if she gets tired, so we leave when she's cranky.

Meanwhile at kid-friendly grandma's house, the carpet is well vacuumed and there are age-appropriate toys. Fragile items are out of reach. Electrical outlets are inaccessible. There's a booster chair strapped to a regular chair, so baby can be fed,

> *Keep kid-friendly snacks on hand like crackers, cheese, fruit, macaroni and cheese, bologna, ham, apple juice, jars of baby food (stages 1, 2, 3), and milk. Even babies starting solids can eat applesauce, macaroni and cheese, crackers (broken up), and apple juice.*

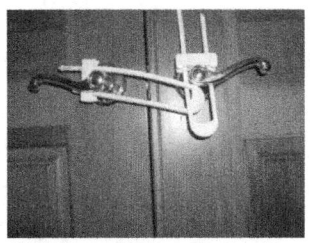

Childproof safety locks for doors and cabinets.

> *Place fragile items out of reach, install outlet covers, lockup medicines, install a staircase, lay carpet or comforter for baby to play, and vacuum floors. Provide a booster or highchair for baby eating solids.*

and there are snacks for older kids when they're hungry. Now, it's not perfect; for example, there's no place for baby to nap, but at least I know that our visit won't include fear of fragile objects, sticking fingers in outlets, or eating nasty bits from the carpet.

2. Provide changing area with diapers and wipes.

Keep a package of diapers and wipes at your house just in case mom or dad forget or run out.

3. Provide baby formula and bottle.

Buy a container of baby formula and bottle for newborn to six mos. (or older depending on baby's age) in case mom or dad forget or don't have enough. Boil bottle and nipple to sterilize, so they're ready when baby needs them.

4. Provide a safe sleeping area for baby, e.g., Moses' basket, bassinet, or playpen, with baby monitor.

Mom and dad will stay longer and have a relaxing visit if there's somewhere to lie baby down when she's tired. Newborns don't have much stamina. In fact, the average newborn sleeps about 16 hours a day.[1] It's impossible to predict when or for how long a newborn will sleep, so it's helpful to provide visiting parents with a safe place where baby can sleep. Shop for a Moses basket, cradle, bassinet, or playpen. A Moses basket is a small padded basket with handles that's a great portable bed for

Top: Gate installed at top of stairs. Bottom: Some gates do not require installation hardware. When gate is positioned between two walls of a stairwell, pressure on a built-in spring keeps it in place.

---

[1] See KidsHealth for Parents:
http://kidshealth.org/parent/growth/sleep/sleepnewborn.html

baby. A bassinet is larger, but also a temporary and safe bed for baby. Playpens fold to a small size making them easy to store, but when opened makes a safe place for baby to sleep. Also, if you set up a baby monitor in your baby sleep area, then mom and dad can hear baby while they relax in another room.

Outlet covers

5. Provide toys for older siblings and baby.

Mom and dad won't look forward to visiting grandma and grandpa if they know they'll have to listen to their kids complain, "I'm bored" or "There's nothing to do." Buy age-appropriate toys. If you have Blu-Ray, streaming, or cable TV, provide age-appropriate kid shows to watch during visits. Art supplies like crayons and paints are terrific for older kids but can be messy and dangerous for baby. Provide them where safe to do so. For baby, supply rattles, teething ring, nested cups, and other age-appropriate toys.

> *Don't let grandkids take toys home. Your toys will keep their interest if they are played with only during visits.*

6. Be ready to pick up and drop off grandkids.

Having your own car seats for your grandkids gives everyone more options. Once your grandkids are safely in car seats, you can drive them to a park, afterschool activities, or a store, and, you can pick them up from school. This makes a visit with grandma and grandpa fit more easily into mom or dad's busy schedule.

One day, for example, grandma called and asked us to come for a visit. "I can't," I said, "It's almost three o'clock, and I still have to make dinner." She replied, "How about you come over in an hour and leave the boys with me so you can go make dinner? I'll bring them home at six o'clock." "Great!" I said. What made this possible were car seats grandma had for my older two sons. Notice also, when confronted by my refusal, she offered a specific suggestion that caused me to consider a new plan, and what a great suggestion because it allowed me to come and visit for a short while with baby, gave me two hours to get dinner ready without my older boys under foot, and provided grandma and grandpa a chance to visit with all three of their grandchildren.

> *Make sure a car seat is age appropriate and installed according to manufacturer instructions. If you have any difficulty installing or using it, return it and try another seat. A well-designed car seat should be easy to install and use.*

7. Offer a meal.

Since preparing a healthy, well-balanced meal takes time, a dinner or lunch offer is a great way to get a visit. Moreover, parents will stay longer knowing that they don't have to rush off to make lunch or dinner for the family.

Chapter Five

Increase Birthday, Holiday, and Special Occasion Visits

1. During a nonholiday time, negotiate a holiday schedule with mom and dad that's fair to you and the other grandparents.

2. Negotiate parts of a holiday rather than the whole celebration.

3. Respect mom and dad's own family traditions.

4. Bring holiday or special occasion dinner to their home.

5. Offer to host the holiday or special occasion celebration.

6. If mom and dad are hosting, ask how you can help by offering specific suggestions like bringing dessert or side dish, providing wine, sitting at the kiddy table.

Getting your share of holiday and special occasion visits with your grandkids can be difficult for a number of reasons. Some grandkids live far away and see their grandparents only once or twice a year, or as is often the case, there's more than one set of grandparents, so mom and dad must decide where to visit during the holidays. Due to divorce and remarriage, in some families there are three or four sets of grandparents wanting visits, and, don't forget, there's also mom and dad to consider. Maybe they want to start their own family traditions and don't want to travel during the holidays?

1. **During a nonholiday time, negotiate a holiday schedule with mom and dad that's fair to you and the other grandparents.**

When holiday expectations don't match, there are arguments, hurt feelings, resentment, and even family feuds. That's why it's important to negotiate your holiday and special occasion expectations with your own son or daughter during a nonholiday time. As we discussed in chapter three "Maintaining a Good Relationship with Mom and Dad," to prevent misunderstandings and arguments negotiate with your blood relative son or daughter not your son-in-law or daughter-in-law. Also, by discussing holiday visit schedules during nonholiday times, you decrease argument and misunderstandings because everyone is less busy and emotions are calmer.

When negotiating a holiday schedule, it's in your best interest to be fair to the other grandparents. Why? Because the fairer the schedule, the more likely it is to be kept. Think of it this way, when a contract between two parties is a great deal for one and not the other, it fails because the party with the bad deal breaches. They're not evil or bad; they simply no longer want to cooperate with an agreement they're not benefitting from. So, you don't want to negotiate a holiday visit schedule that's great for you, but isn't for the other grandparents or the parents themselves because it won't last, and you're likely to end up with misunderstandings, arguments, and hurt feelings.

If there's only one other set of grandparents, suggest to mom and dad that you alternate holidays every year. For instance, this year you get Thanksgiving and they get Christmas. Next year you reverse it. This type of schedule works well for most families; however, if there's more than two sets of grandparents, things are more complicated. You can still try to divide the holidays between grandparents and rotate who hosts what holiday over the years, or you could try to negotiate parts of the holidays.

2. Negotiate parts of a holiday rather than the whole celebration.

A good way to get your share of holiday visits is to negotiate parts of a holiday rather than the whole celebration. Holidays have a few mini celebrations or traditions within them. If your grandkids are at the other grandparents' home for Easter dinner, for example, then how about coloring eggs or hosting an Easter egg hunt at a different time? Similarly, if other grandparents are taking kids to fireworks on Fourth of July, why not suggest taking them to a parade or hosting a BBQ?

Early in my marriage, I was at my mother-in-law's for dinner. The subject of the holidays came up. I asked whether one of her sons and his family were going to visit for Christmas. "Oh yes, they'll be with us for Christmas," she replied. Knowing they had other grandparents in town, I asked, "Will they be with us for Christmas Eve, morning, or dinner?" I was surprised by how immediate and certain my mother-in-law was. "Well of course they'll be here for all of it," she said. "Are you sure?" I asked. "Don't they want to spend even a part of the holiday with their other relatives?" As it turned out some months later, they spent Christmas Eve and morning at the other grandparent's home and then drove thirty minutes to have Christmas Dinner at my mother-in-law's. Splitting up holiday events makes so much sense, but it surprised me that the possibility hadn't occurred to my mother-in-law.

> *Negotiate parts of a holiday: Christmas Eve, Christmas Morning, Christmas Dinner, Easter Egg Coloring, Easter Egg Hunt, Easter Dinner, New Year's Eve, New Year's Day, Pumpkin Carving, Trick or Treating, Fourth of July Parade, Fourth of July BBQ, Fourth of July Fireworks, Thanksgiving Day Parade, Thanksgiving Dinner.*

3. Respect mom and dad's own family traditions.

At some point most families want to establish their own family traditions. They want their kids to wake up to their own Christmas tree, for example, or celebrate Thanksgiving with mom's turkey and stuffing. If you're a grandma or grandpa that's gotten used to hosting the holidays

> *If your son or daughter wants to host the holiday feast in their home, maybe you should just bring a dessert or side dish and pull up a chair?*

with everyone gathering at your home, it may be time to pass the baton to the next generation. If your daughter or daughter-in-law wants to cook the holiday feast for her family at her house, consider simply bringing over a dessert or side dish and pulling up a chair.

If you're a long-distance grandparent and mom and dad want to stay home for the holidays, suggest that they travel to see you at a nonholiday time each year. When my first child was a baby, we traveled from California to Massachusetts at Christmas time to visit my mom. We did it again after my second son was born, but thereafter I decided that I wanted my kids to wake up with their own Christmas tree each year. Knowing my mom would be heartbroken by this decision, we promised to fly to see her for two weeks each summer. Now, if my mom wants to see us during the holidays, she flies to us (less expensive and easier for just one person to travel during the holidays). We're all happy.

4. Bring holiday or special occasion dinner to their home.

Often with a new baby there are special eating requirements and nap schedules that make going to someone else's home for dinner difficult. Mom and dad may have to gulp down dinner in a hurry to get baby home to bed, or maybe they didn't bring enough diapers? Often for a young family, it's hard to find time to host a holiday meal. There's so much to cook and clean which is difficult to do with young children.

Why not offer to bring the holiday meal to their home? That way, diapers, infant/toddler food, crib, and highchair are there and mom and dad can relax and enjoy the meal without rushing out the door. I vividly remember the shouts of joy when grandma, my mother's mom, arrived for Easter dinner carrying crispy duck, pie, mashed turnips, potatoes, and string beans. My brother, sister and I were 8, 6, and 1 years old. It was a wonderful time.

5. Offer to host the holiday or special occasion celebration.

If your grandkids are a bit older and no longer need naps or special food, then consider offering to host the holiday meal. I really love when my mother-in-law does this. My husband keeps complaining that we need to start having holiday dinners at our home, but I keep putting him off. It's so much work to cook and clean up after a big meal, and with my three kids' busy schedules, it's a relief to let someone else host.

6. If mom and dad are hosting, ask how you can help by offering specific suggestions like bringing dessert or side dish, providing wine, sitting at the kiddy table.

As discussed earlier a few chapters ago, if you ask, "How can I help?" and leave it at that you're likely to get a polite knee-jerk response like: "That's okay, I don't need anything." Try offering specific suggestions instead like: "Can I bring dessert?" or "How about I make the candied yams?" or "I'll bring the wine" or "Can I sit at the kiddie table and help with the kids?" Specific suggestions offer possibilities that parents may not have considered. If they continue to insist that they don't need anything, then just bring yourself and pull up a chair.

Chapter Six

When Things are too Good at Grandma's: How to Get Less Visits

1. Gently remind mom and dad that you have your own life.

2. Use the call-before-visit rule.

3. Set an easily remembered visit day.

Sometimes things are too good at Grandma's! You may feel like there are too many babysit requests or that your generosity is being exploited, and you're probably right. With the increase in single parent households, grandma and grandpa are needed more than ever. According to 2020 census data, 25% of children in the US live in single parent households. When there's only one parent, there's no one to hand baby off to. This can understandably put pressure on grandma and grandpa for frequent babysits. Consider, for example, the plight of a California grandma who babysits her granddaughter while her daughter works full-time. Within months of starting the arrangement, her daughter called from work to say she'd be late and asked her mom to make dinner. Sometimes she'd call on weekends for babysits, and other times she'd just show up. What bothered grandma was her daughter's sense of entitlement. As she described it, "I'm a 24-hour baby-sitting service. The idea that I have plans doesn't enter her head." She summed up her predicament this way, "Here my daughter is a parent, and I still have to set limits for her!"

> *Explain to mom or dad why they can't visit. An explanation reassures them that they've done nothing wrong, while reminding them that you have your own obligations.*

1. Gently remind mom and dad that you have your own life.

If mom and dad rely on you a little too much, then it's time to set limits. Say no firmly and politely with gentle reminders that you have your own obligations. Sometimes it's hard for mom and dad to remember that their parents have their own busy lives, and an explanation can take the sting out of saying "no" by reassuring them that it's not anything they did wrong.

2. Use the call-before-visit rule.

If too many unannounced visits are a problem, explain to mom and dad that you love seeing them but would rather they call before coming by. Explain why—you may have other plans or might not be feeling well, for example. Again, providing an explanation reassures them that it's not anything they've done wrong while gently reminding them that you have your own life.

3. Set an easily remembered visit day.

Setting an easily remembered visit day, like every Thursday for example, is another good way to reduce babysit requests and surprise visits. Explain to mom and dad that this helps them too because now they can schedule their errands for that day without having to consult with you. Set a date that's easy for everyone to remember like, for example, Tuesday afternoons at grandpa's house or every other Thursday afternoon at the playground.

> *A weekly "visit day" can help parents restrict errands for which they need a sitter to a single day thereby decreasing requests for you to babysit.*

Additionally, setting a grandma or grandpa visit day helps mom and dad quiet grandkids who pester them to go to grandma and grandpa's house, for example, "Not today. It isn't a grandma and grandpa day" or "We're going over Friday that's enough; let's not go over today."

Chapter Seven

Long-Distance Grandparenting

1. Arrange as many visits per year as time and money permit.

2. Use easy-to-use technology.

3. Provide mom and dad 9x11 self-addressed envelopes to mail grandkids' artwork to you.

4. Write to your grandchildren via US mail.

5. Suggest a weekend, week, or month with grandma and grandpa during the summer.

Living in a different state, country, or a distant part of the same state may make it difficult to maintain a presence in your grandchildren's lives. Frankly, nothing can replace the close, personal interaction that visits provide; therefore, you should arrange them whenever time and money permit. However, if only one or two visits per year are possible, there are many other ways to maintain a close bond.

1. Arrange as many visits per year as time and money permit.

If you can't afford to see your grandchildren as much as you want, then say so. Mom and dad may have solutions and, even if they don't right away, telling them puts them on the lookout for opportunities that arise. For example, say you've decided that you'd like to see your grandkids every six months but can't afford to fly to see them that often. If you tell mom and dad, they may be able to help you get a visit by contributing toward a plane ticket or arranging a family vacation nearby your location, or maybe they have frequent flyer miles or credit card points to buy a ticket? There are lots of possibilities.

> *If you can't afford to see your grandchildren as much as you'd like, say so! This puts mom and dad on the lookout for opportunities to help.*

One year, we were unable to do our annual summer vacation in Cape Cod because of a conflict. My mom told me she was upset because she relied on us vacationing there to see her grandchildren. As it turned out, we also planned a Disneyworld vacation in Florida later that year, so my husband and I bought grandma a plane ticket to come along. She was thrilled to run around the Magic Kingdom with her grandkids! But if grandma hadn't voiced her unhappiness, we would not have thought to take her to Disney.

> *If you use a credit card for purchases, consider switching to one that accumulates frequent flyer miles. Charge as many of your daily expenses as possible so that you build up miles for free flights or reduced-price tickets.*

2. Use easy-to-use technology.

In 2019, eighty-eight percent of Americans age 50-64 and seventy-three percent over age 65 regularly used the internet.[2] Their laptop and smartphone helped them stay close to family and particularly family living far away. If you don't have a laptop or smartphone, consider buying one. Other family members are video calling and texting back and forth exchanging stories, making plans, sharing photos and making memories. This is all passing you by.

> *Another great option is instant message ("IM"). With IM you can type back and forth in real time. You can also set up a friends list that shows you when your grandkids are online. Google Chat, Facebook Messenger, and Yahoo Messenger are among the most popular, free IM services.*

In our family, we have a grandma that doesn't have a smartphone. When we see her at holiday dinners, she often feels left out because she's the last to hear family news. She's missed important family announcements sent via text like graduation and birthday plans, travel plans, and new jobs. This isn't intentional—family members send texts and forget she isn't part of it. During holiday dinners she catches up on what the rest of us have been texting and video calling about.

Your grandchildren began using laptops and smartphones as early as kindergarten to play games, do homework, chat with friends, contact teachers, shop for music and clothes, join sports clubs, etc. As they grow, they carry their cell phones with them everywhere. Thanks to this easy-to-use technology, you can be in contact with them any time of day. Texting on smartphones is free with most plans and always free if you use WiFi, for example, with iPhone's iMessage. You can also text photos and videos to each other, or you can video call using FaceTime, Facebook messenger video chat, or Zoom on your smartphone or laptop.

With high-tech communication, your grandkids can instantly reply to your messages. They can ask your advice any time they need it and text links for you to click on about whatever they're interested in. You can watch movies, sports, or play video games together on

---

[2]https://www.statista.com/statistics/266587/percentage-of-internet-users-by-age-groups-in-the-us/ 2019

your smartphone or laptop. In fact, a survey by PopCap Games found that millions of grandparents, particularly grandmas, play computer games with their grandkids, and 95% of these computer gaming grandmas said the games helped them "bond with, or better relate to" their grandchildren.[3] But if the computer games your grandkids play aren't what you're used to, suggest chess, checkers, or a card game online. Your grandkids probably have even more ideas of how to keep in touch using the Web—ask them.

Canny grannies are tech savvy. They're favorites because they understand their grandkids' world and interact within it. If you find the prospect of becoming a "techno granny" daunting, ask family members to help you select a smartphone and set up WiFi. Remember, this isn't difficult for them. They have their own smartphones and know what to do. They'll be happy to help.

3. Provide mom and dad 9x11 self-addressed envelopes to mail grandkids' artwork to you.

Kids create art at school, home, girl scouts, boy scouts, summer camp, and afterschool programs. There's so much that parents throw a lot away. Instead, suggest mom and dad send artwork to you. "There's nothing more wonderful than seeing the picture my granddaughter drew hanging on the refrigerator," a Florida grandma told me. "It's so bright and happy just like she is!" Make it easy for mom and dad by offering a supply of 9 x 11 self-addressed envelopes. The easier you make it, the more often you'll receive your grandkid's art.

Consider giving a small empty photo or scrapbook album to your grandkids. Ask them to fill it with pictures, notes, and drawings to send to you.

4. Write to your grandchildren via US mail.

We've talked a lot about keeping in touch using technology because that's what your grandkids are used to; however, it's exciting for kids to receive cards and letters via US mail because they seldom get them. The process of communication is slower than they're used to with texting and instant messaging, but they'll

---

[3] See http://seniorjournal.com/NEWS/Grandparents/2007/7-08-31-Millions.html.

love experiencing how you communicated when you were their age. Running to the mailbox to read cards and letters will spark conversations about visits, phone calls, and writing back.

5. Suggest a weekend, week, or month at grandma's during the summer.

If your grandkids are old enough to travel, suggest a week or weekend at your home. The best time is when school is out during the summer. Kids are driving mom and dad crazy looking for things to do. Maybe mom or dad can drop them off or they can travel by train, bus, or plane? Even just a weekend visit with grandma or grandpa can have a big impact.

One summer when I was eight-years-old, my mom drove me to Providence, Rhode Island to stay with my grandma for a week. While there, grandma took me to the beach, helped me practice piano, taught me some new table manners, took me clothes shopping, and cooked with me. I remember how she never actually went to bed at night; she'd wander about the house and occasionally fall asleep in a chair. She explained she'd always slept that way since she was little. She loved Hershey chocolate bars with almonds and ate one each day. She hated the taste of coffee and refused to drink it. We talked about how funny it was that her birthday was on April Fool's Day. We spent time tending her tomato plants and rose bushes. I have strong memories of her because of that extended visit.

My other grandma was local and dropped by my house once or twice a month, but I don't remember her as clearly as the grandma I lived with. This demonstrates how long-distance grandparents can be spiritually closer to their grandkids than local ones. It's about the quality of time spent. Extended visit opportunities give your grandkids a chance to be a part of your home, routine, habits, customs, and hobbies without the interruption of mom or dad.

A study by the University of Florida found that "grandtravel," the practice of kids and their grandparents vacationing together without parents, was becoming increasingly popular among seniors who like to "spoil the grandchild without interference from the parents." Nearly 80% of grandparents surveyed endorsed the practice.[4] And, why not? Grandtravel seems to benefit everyone. Grandparents and their grandkids spend quality time together, and mom and dad are secure knowing that their kids are with family. Some of the more popular grandtravel destinations include trips to theme parks and historic sites.[5]

As your grandkids grow up, there will be a limited number of extended or overnight visit opportunities, so you'll want to make the most of them. Before they arrive, decide what you want from the visit. What do you want them to know and remember most about you? Would visits to Disneyland and Sea World accomplish that? Or, would it be better to do what my grandma so wisely did—simply share her daily routine? Even our two beach days together were spent at a beach that meant a lot to her—she used to take her own children (including my dad) there. I love my grandma for this. Two years later, when I was ten, my dad (her son) unexpectedly died. My mom eventually remarried, and I didn't see much of my grandma after that, but I still treasure the memory of that summer week we spent together long ago.

---

[4]See http://seniorjournal.com/NEWS/Travel/6-07-25-GrandtravelPopular.html.

[5]Ibid.

Chapter Eight

Create Meaningful Shared Experiences

1. Read what your grandkids read.

2. Start a collection together.

3. Share recipes and cook with your grandkids.

4. Watch their favorite television shows.

5. Share your garden and help them start their own.

6. Volunteer in your grandchild's classroom or coach their sports team.

We're the sum of our experiences. As a grandparent, you've got a lot to share. Sharing your past with your grandkids is fun but will never be as memorable as what you do together. It's time you share that they'll treasure most. It doesn't matter if you're a local or long-distance grandparent; there are plenty of things you can do to create special memories together.

1. Read what your grandkids read.

Your grandkids are required to read at least 30 minutes a day by their elementary school. When they reach middle and high school, they're required to read much more. Ask your grandkids what they're reading and read it too. Buy it on Amazon or check it out from your local library. Discuss the book as you read it, and you'll learn a lot about each other while sharing your points of view.

> *A good book inspires conversations that challenge and change young lives—perfect for the wisdom of grandma and grandpa.*

One summer, I formed a book club with my oldest son called, creatively enough, "Mom's Book Club." I did it because I thought he was reading too many comic books. That summer we read two books" "Stone Fox" and "Johnny Tremain." "Stone Fox" turned out to have a sad, heart-wrenching ending about a boy's dog dying while helping to save the family farm. My son and I discussed sacrifice, friendship, and perseverance. Years later, he still talks to me about that book, and while reading "Johnny Tremain," we had conversations about colonial New England, minute men, the revolutionary war, dying for your country, and how a young man decides what to do with his life. These are the kinds of conversations that challenge and change young lives—perfect for the wisdom of grandma and grandpa.

If the book you're reading together is part of their homework, offer to help with a book report or other school project. When summer comes, pick books together and form your own book club. If you're buying books, donate them to your grandkids' school or your library when you're done. Put a short inscription inside each one about your book club, and you'll inspire others.

2. Start a collection together.

Starting a collection with your grandchild is a clever way to give them insight into who you are, where you live, and what you like. Think about your favorite foods, activities, hobbies and consider what you could collect together: models, matchbox cars, stamps, comics, baseball cards, state quarters, plants, recipes, and more. It's a lot of fun.

My kids' grandpa shared his coin collection. Of his three grandkids, one was interested, so Grandpa helped him get started. Now they have great fun collecting coins and discussing their collections.

How about helping a grandchild get started by giving a collection as a gift? When my daughter was born, her great grandma gave her a collection of six dolls from around the world. We mounted a shelf in her room to display them. It's great grandma's hope that she'll add to it as she grows up. The dolls make a beautiful display that mesmerizes little girls who come over to play. My daughter proudly tells them, "GG gave them to me when I was a baby."

Collecting doesn't have to be expensive or complicated. One of my sons started collecting wine corks that his dad and I gave him. His local and long-distance grandparents found out about it and began collecting them too. They enjoy trading the exotic ones and discussing the countries they come from. Every once and a while, we'll get an envelope full of corks from his far away grandparents. That's always exciting because the corks are from bottles not commonly found in our area. My kid's grandparents also help them collect state quarters and cactus plants.

3. Share recipes and cook with your grandkids.

If you enjoy cooking, this is a wonderful way to get quality time with your grandchildren. Most grandmas and grandpas have a few things that they make that are family favorites. In my family, our local grandma's prime rib, spaetzle, seven-layer cake, and chimichangas are family favorites. Our long-distance grandma's turkey stuffing, fried spinach, brownies, pies, and fried chicken are the bomb. Imagine what would happen if these two women suddenly died without passing on their secrets? These family favorites would go with them if not passed on to the next generation.

When I was little, my local grandma made the most delicious crispy duck. Even if the holiday main course was something else, she would breeze in with a couple of ducks to add. When I was a teenager, she died of cancer. When we gathered for our first holiday without her, we suddenly realized that we'd never taste her crispy duck again. We searched her kitchen for the recipe but couldn't find it. We tried to recreate it from the way we remember it tasting but didn't succeed. Grandma's crispy duck lives only in my memory now; I wish I could share it with my kids.

Make a recipe book or box of family favorites and give it to your grandkids, or you can add your recipes to a recipe box app for your smartphone or laptop and share it with your grandkids. In our family, we use an app called RecipeBox on our iPhones (downloaded for free from the Apple app store) to share recipes. Whenever we're in a supermarket and want to make grandma's brownies, cookies, stuffing or other recipes, all we have to do is open the app on our iPhone and the ingredients are there showing us what to buy.

> *Kids love to cook. Pass on family favorites by cooking together.*

As your grandkids grow, give them cooking lessons. If you're a long-distance grandma, Zoom call or FaceTime and cook together. When I was twelve-years-old, the grandma who made the great crispy duck gave me a birthday card in which she promised to come to my house and teach me how to make pie crust. We spent four hours together one afternoon cooking and eating the results. It's a memory I cherish, and my kids, her great grandchildren, eat her pies every holiday. When the kids help me bake, I tell them about their "expert pie making" great grandma, and how I long to taste her crispy duck again.

4. Watch their favorite television shows.

Ask your grandkids what shows they like to watch. Some may be ones you watch too. Many of the shows kids like are a lot of fun.

Some are more thought provoking than others, however, and you may be able to help steer them in a better direction.

We have a grandma who watches "Survivor" and "The Amazing Race," so she can FaceTime with her grandkids about them. They enjoy discussing the different countries and cultures featured on the shows. They also share strategy and speculate about who they think will win. Grandma started watching these shows because she heard her grandkids discuss them. And, one of my sons is crazy about the science show "Nova." His grandpa streams it so they can discuss it. It's a relief for my son to talk with someone in the family who understands this stuff—I'm not a science or math person. Now, he turns to his grandpa with all sorts of scientific questions.

Another way to share TV time with your grandkids is to FaceTime or Zoom using your laptop or phone while watching a movie or TV show. TV streaming service SlingTV recently added a feature called "watch party" with which subscribers can invite three people to watch a movie or TV show with them. It's like a Zoom or FaceTime call that includes a movie or TV show. Amazon and NetFlix also have a watch party feature, but the video chat is not built in so use Zoom or FaceTime along with it.

5. Share your garden and help them start their own.

If you have a garden, share it with your grandkids. My daughter loves walking through grandma's garden. It's just a few rose bushes, but she delights in making bouquets to bring home. She often helps grandma plant, weed, and water. When I was eight, one of my fondest memories of grandma was helping her tend tomato plants. She taught me the importance of water, sunlight, tomato cages, hornworms, and weeding. Our long-distance grandparents have a greenhouse with cherry tomatoes, kiwi, and oranges. They send seedlings to encourage their grandkids to plant their own garden. Sprouting seeds in small peat pots is a terrific way to introduce kids to the wonders of growing things. When grandma and grandpa visit, they help their grandkids plant their seedlings in the garden. They learn to

> *Sprouting seeds in small peat pots on the window sill is a great way to introduce kids to the wonders of growing things.*

appreciate nature and the outdoors while sharing it all with grandma and grandpa.

6. Volunteer in your grandchild's classroom or coach their sports team.

The best way to get involved in your grandchild's daily routine and meet their friends is to be a classroom volunteer. Volunteers are welcome from kindergarten through 7th or 8th grade, and schools need them. You can help with reading, writing, grading papers, and assisting with projects. My mother-in-law volunteered in my son's kindergarten class each week, and he loved it. Now my son is eleven, and grandma still asks about his friends she met in his kindergarten class—many of them are still in his classes in 6th grade! When they come over to hang out and play video games, grandma knows them and they remember her too!

Your community recreational soccer, basketball, and baseball teams are looking for volunteer coaches and assistant coaches. Depending on the age group, you may even be able to request that your grandkid's friends be on the team. Even if you and your grandchild don't know anyone else on the team, you'll quickly make friends with parents and kids. Friends they make here show up on teams next year and in their classrooms at school, and there's the fun, hard work, and pride that comes with practice and teamplay. The wisdom of grandma and grandpa are perfect for lessons they'll learn about working hard, teamwork, winning, and losing.

Chapter Nine

Thoughtful Gifts that Resonate

1. Give your grandkids books and games that you enjoyed as a child. Include a note explaining why it's special to you

2. Make a photo album or scrapbook for your grandkids.

3. Give your grandchild the gift of grandma or grandpa for a day.

4. Create a memory to display in their room.

5. Make them a keepsake to use during the holidays.

Spoiling grandkids is more than just a cliché—it's a favorite pass time, and why not? Grandkids love it, and there's always time with mom and dad for rules and discipline. Grandma and grandpa time is fun time, and favorite grandparents also make it meaningful and memorable. Giving thoughtful gifts that resonate is what this chapter is about.

1. Give your grandkids books and games you enjoyed as a child. Include a note explaining why it's special to you.

It's fun for kids to imagine their grandparents were once their age. Giving them books and games you enjoyed as a child is a thoughtful way to share your childhood memories and spark conversations. "Can we play the game that grandpa played when he was little?" or "Let's read the book that was grandma's favorite when she was my age?"

Games and books from grandma or grandpa accompanied by a note explaining why it's your favorite are enthusiastically enjoyed time and again by grandkids eager to discover what makes this toy or book so special. "How old was grandpa when he played this?" "Did grandpa this to you before you went to bed, dad? "Did grandma play this with you, mom, when you were little?"

> *Giving your grandchildren books and games that you enjoyed as a child is a thoughtful way to share your fondest childhood memories.*

2. Make a photo album or scrapbook for your grandkids.

Kids love to look through photo albums and talk about their adventures with grandma and grandpa. Looking at photos recalls special times and helps when family members miss each other; it also makes grandkids eager for your next visit. Consider including photos of yourself with your son or daughter as little ones. Write a couple of sentences about what their mom or dad were like as kids. Looking through the album will inspire conversations about what mom, dad, grandma, and grandpa liked to do, how much fun grandma and grandpa are, how much they miss you, when they will see you next, or when to call you. Don't forget to include your phone number, mail and email address in the album, so your grandkids can easily text, call, or write.

Photo albums or scrapbooks can be a great comfort for to those who miss you or other family members. After returning home from a visit to see her grandkids in California, my mom filled a small album with pictures from the visit and mailed it to us. In the album were photos of our family cat playing with her and the kids. A few months later, our cat died. I didn't have any recent pictures of the cat—only a few taken when she was a kitten. My kids carried grandma's album around the house looking at the photos of them playing with the cat. It was a great comfort to them to look through grandma's album at that sad time.

3. Give your grandchild the gift of grandma or grandpa for a day.

This gift will resonate throughout their life because it's a gift of a meaningful, shared experience. Ask your grandchild what they would like to do most, and then do it with them. Whatever it might be. If they don't have any idea or ask you to suggest something, then offer things that will create a meaningful memory. Cooking, knitting, gardening, fishing, or hanging out with grandma or grandpa while you go through your daily routine. Maybe there's something you're known for in the family that your grandkids would love to learn about? Here's an opportunity for grandma or grandpa to reveal their secrets! How about a gift of an overnight or weekend visit? One birthday, my son's grandfather took him fishing off a pier. His grandpa had asked him what he wanted to do, and he asked to fish. Dad and his brother tagged along, and they pier fished together. It's a favorite birthday memory.

Whatever you suggest, remember, it's their choice. Don't force them to do what you want and don't be disappointed if they pick something you didn't suggest. This is their gift; whatever they decide to do with you will make a fine memory.

4. Create a memory to display in their room.

Consider creating memories for your grandkid's room. Kids spend a lot of time there playing, pretending, entertaining friends, getting away from their parents, texting, listening to music, doing homework, resting, and reflecting. I'm sure you remember the many hours you spent in your room as you grew up?

On her bedroom wall, one of my kids has a framed sewing sampler from her grandma containing her name and date of birth. It's a beautiful keepsake that I know she'll take with her when she's out on her own. The same grandma also created a framed sewing sampler for the kids' bathroom that says, "My Other Bathroom is Cleaner." It gives the kids a chuckle when they go in there. Grandpa helped my boys decorate their room by buying large, block-shaped stamps of dinosaurs, frogs, and bugs. They then spent a day stamping a border around the room using latex paint. After he returned home, grandpa sent a framed picture of their painting day for the boys to hang on their wall.

> *Buy a kit online or from a craft store to make something together like a mobile, wall hanging, or decorative box*

You could also make things together. I bought a decorative butterfly kit for my daughter that sat in its box for weeks until grandma asked to make it with her. Now it hangs prominently on my daughter's wall. She often mentions how much fun it was to make it with grandma, or you could paint a jewelry box and put jewelry you'd like to pass down in the box. How about decorating a frame with seashells or stones you collect and putting a photo of the two of you in it, or how about helping start a collection? As I mentioned in the previous chapter, my daughter's great grandma gave her a collection of dolls from around the world. They're displayed on a shelf in her room. My daughter says she drifts to sleep admiring them.

5. Make them a keepsake to use during the holidays.

Keepsakes can become a special part of your grandchild's holiday traditions that they'll look forward to year after year. When I was a little girl, my Jewish grandma made needlepoint Christmas stockings for my brother, sister, and me. Each was unique, colorful, and beautifully detailed. They quickly replaced the store-bought ones we'd been using. After we grew up, we each took our stockings with us. During my first Christmas with my husband, I hung up my favorite stocking. He was jealous, so I needlepointed one for him. As our kids grew, they wanted their own too. I bought Christmas stockings and decorated them with beads, stick-on foam letters to make their names, snowflakes, and more. Each one is a unique work of art. At Christmas time, my kids insist on hanging their own stockings. Someday when they grow up, they'll share them with their own families and continue the tradition of making Christmas stockings. Just look at what their great grandma started! She died years before my kids were born, and yet each Christmas they share the story of their great grandma and the stocking she made that started the tradition as they admire their own.

Think about what kind of holiday keepsake you could create for your grandkids. Maybe you and your grandkids could make a keepsake together? Perhaps an ornament or cup or plate to hold a snack for Santa? An advent calendar? How about decorating Easter baskets to use on the family hunt? Halloween decorations? Hanukkah celebration or decorations? Shop for craft materials online or at your local craft store.

Chapter Ten

Stay the Favorite

How do you stay the favorite? As time goes by, mom and dad will change jobs, move, divorce, re-marry, have more children, and gain stepchildren, but if you follow the simple suggestions discussed in this book, you'll continue to have plenty of visits with your grandkids. Here are the basics to keep in mind.

1. The easier you make it for mom and dad to visit, the more they will. For more about this, go to Chapter One "Get Ready for Grandbaby" and Chapter Two "Help at Birth and with the Newborn."

2. Maintain a good relationship with mom and dad by dealing with your own relatives and respecting mom and dad's decisions. For more about this, go to Chapter Three "Maintain a Good Relationship with Mom and Dad."

3. When you want more visits, offer specific suggestions to provide mom and dad with possibilities. For more about this, go to Chapter Four "Get More Visits."

4. Negotiate parts of a holiday instead of the whole to reduce stress on mom and dad and other grandparents. For more about this, go to Chapter Five "Increase Birthday, Holiday, and Special Occasion Visits."

5. Use text messages, Zoom, FaceTime, Facebook messenger video chat, and instant messages to stay close to your grandkids and do favorite things together like read books, watch movies/TV, share a collection, create art projects, exchange photos, and arrange weekend or week-long visits

during the summer. For more, go to Chapter Seven "Long-Distance Grandparenting."

6. Plan meaningful activities and gifts that convey who you are, for example, give a book or game you enjoyed as a child, make a memory to display in your grandchild's room, create a family tradition, or give a keepsake to use during holidays. For more, go to Chapter Eight "Create Meaningful Shared Experiences" and Chapter Nine "Thoughtful Gifts that Resonate.

About the Author

Attorney turned award-winning author Elizabeth Gardner has been coaching students into selective colleges like the University of Virginia, the University of North Carolina Chapel Hill, Duke University, Princeton University, Yale University, and the University of Cambridge since 2008. Her books *Coach Mom Top College Admission Playbook* and *Standing Out by Stepping Back The Zen of Getting Into Selective Colleges* were published in 2020 and 2023.

A successful author in the parenting genre, her books *Crib Sheets New Parent Sleep Solutions* and *Canny Granny How to Be the Favorite Grandparent* are Mom's Choice Award® recipients. Elizabeth lives a happy, quiet life in Weaverville, North Carolina.

Made in the USA
Monee, IL
01 May 2025